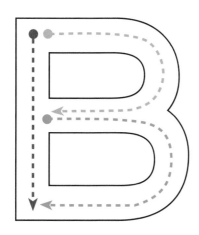

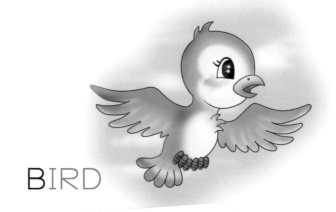

BIRD

書一畫
Trace the Lines

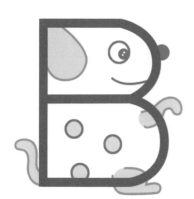 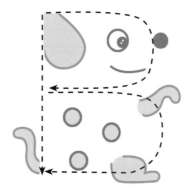 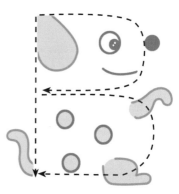

寫一寫
Trace and write

B B B B

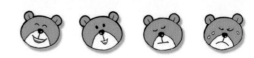

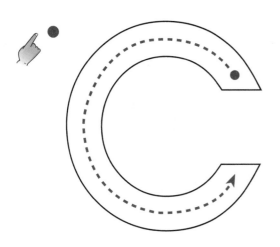

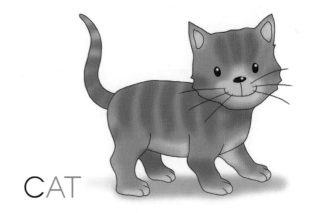

CAT

書一畫

Trace the Lines

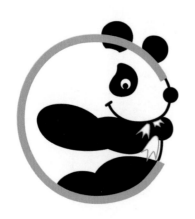 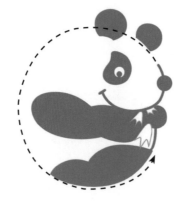 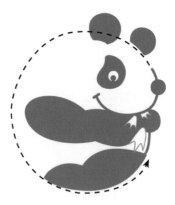

寫一寫

Trace and write

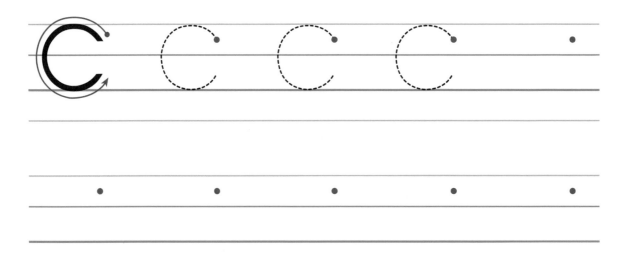

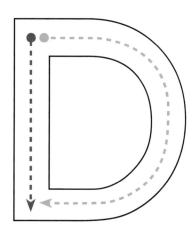

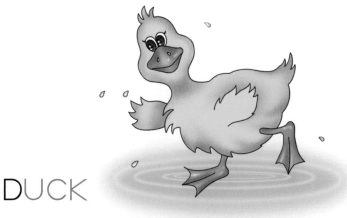

DUCK

書一畫
Trace the Lines

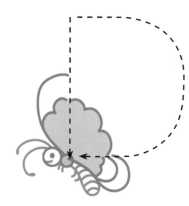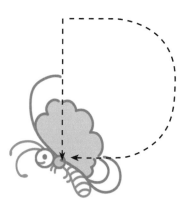

寫一寫
Trace and write

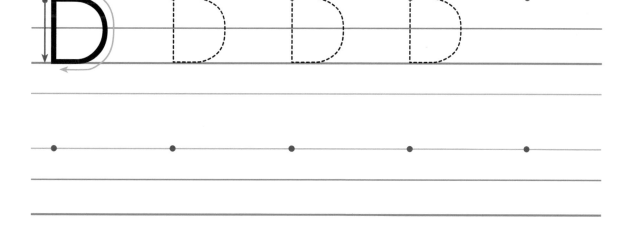

5

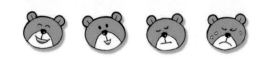

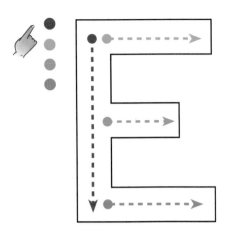

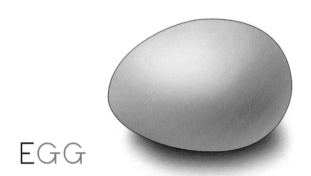

EGG

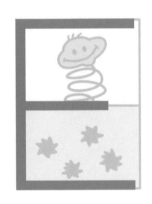
畫一畫
Trace the Lines

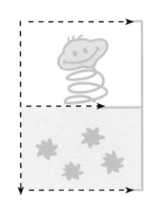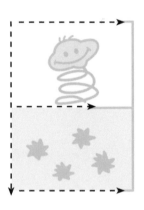

寫一寫
Trace and write

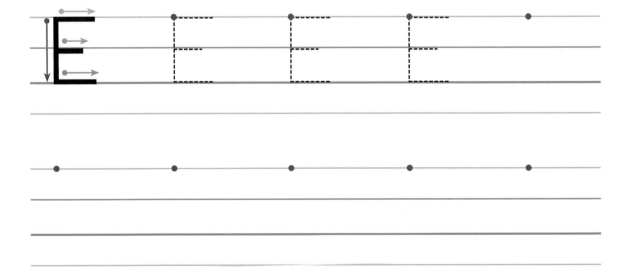

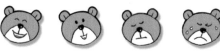

配 對
Matching

CAT •⋯⋯⋯⋯⋯⋯⋯⋯⋯⋯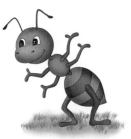

BIRD •

DUCK •

ANT •

EGG •

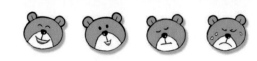

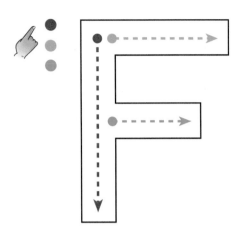

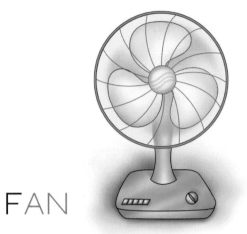

FAN

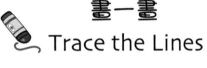

畫一畫
Trace the Lines

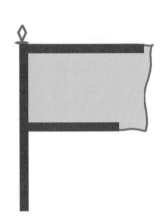

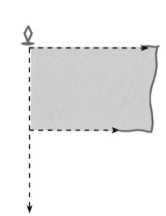

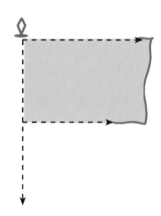

寫一寫
Trace and write

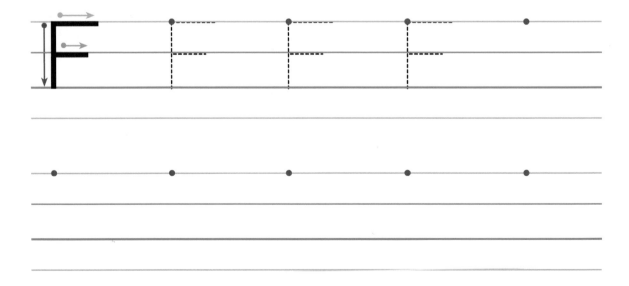

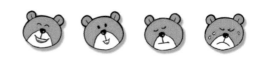

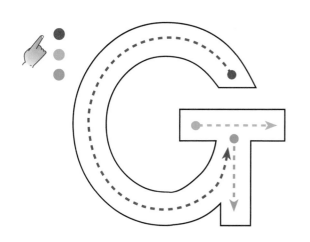

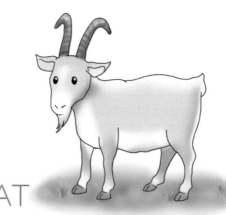

GOAT

 畫一畫
Trace the Lines

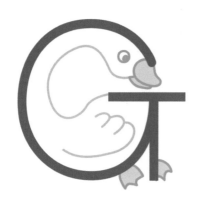 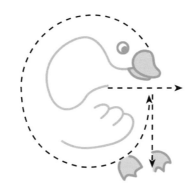 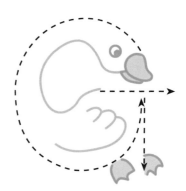

寫一寫
Trace and write

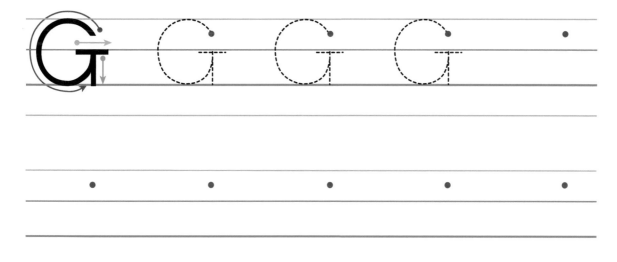

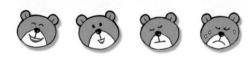

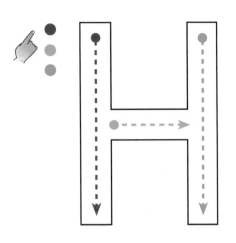

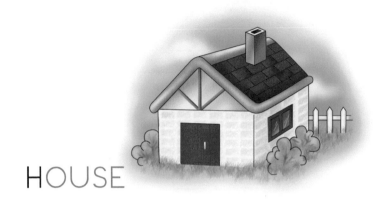

HOUSE

書一畫
Trace the Lines

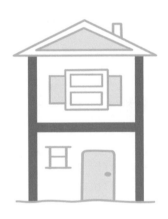

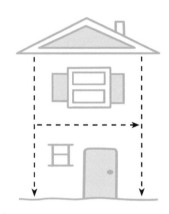

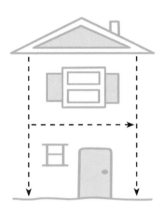

寫一寫
Trace and write

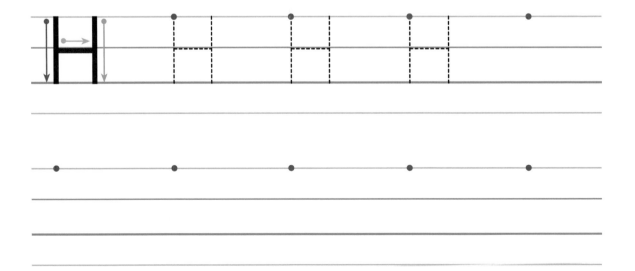

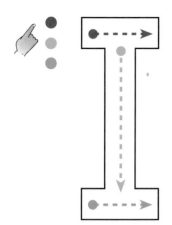

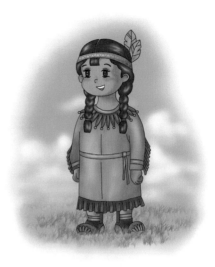

INDIAN

畫一畫
Trace the Lines

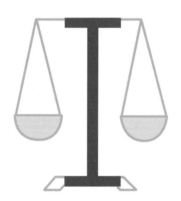 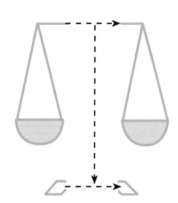 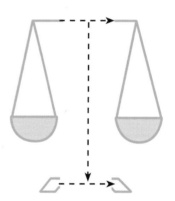

寫一寫
Trace and write

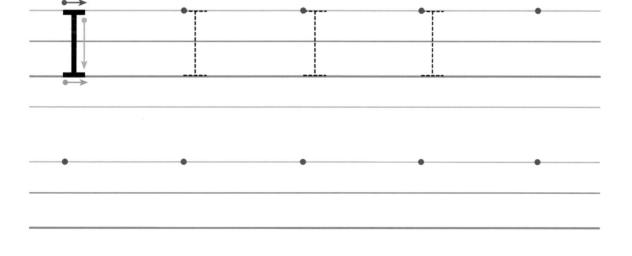

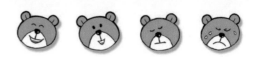

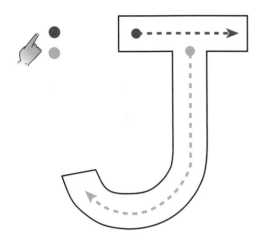

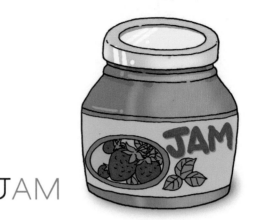

JAM

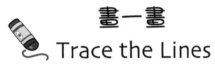

畫一畫
Trace the Lines

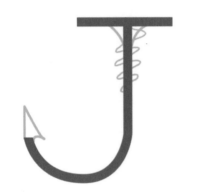
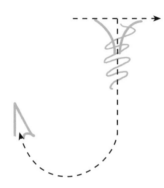
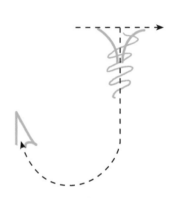

寫一寫
Trace and write

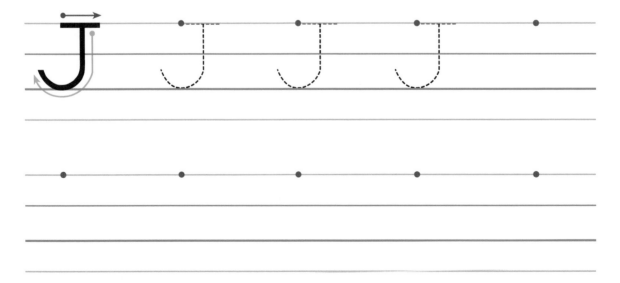

請圈出正確的圖畫。
Please circle the correct pictures.

FAN	
GOAT	
HOUSE	
INDIAN	
JAM	

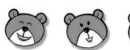

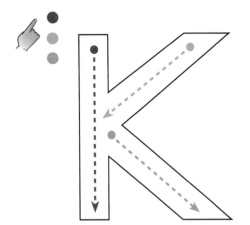

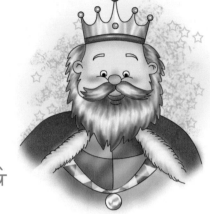

KING

畫一畫
Trace the Lines

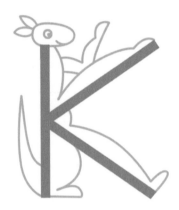 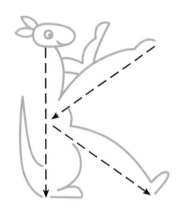 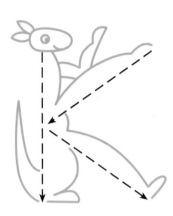

寫一寫
Trace and write

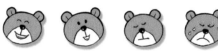

 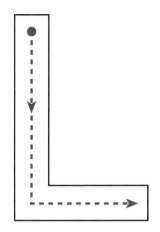

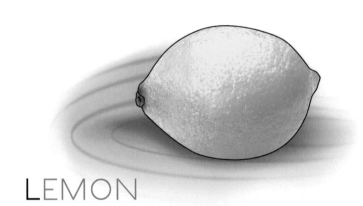

LEMON

 畫一畫
Trace the Lines

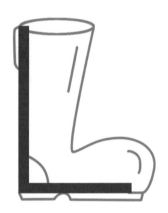 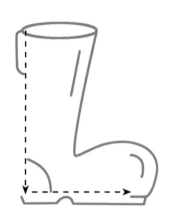 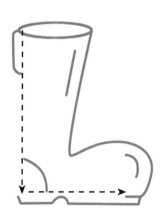

寫一寫
Trace and write

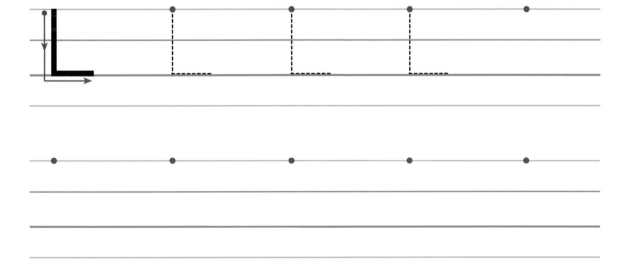

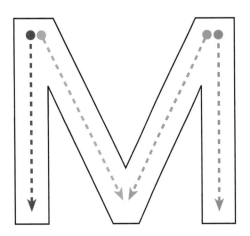

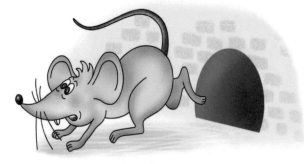

MOUSE

 畫一畫

Trace the Lines

 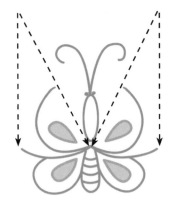 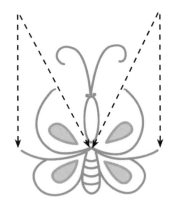

 寫一寫

Trace and write

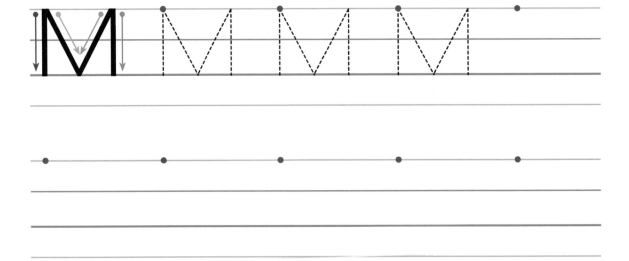

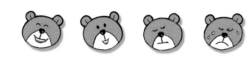

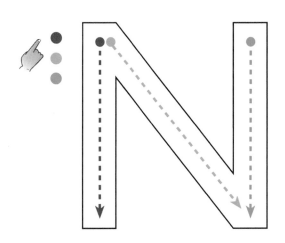

N OSE

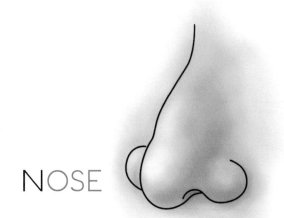

書一畫
Trace the Lines

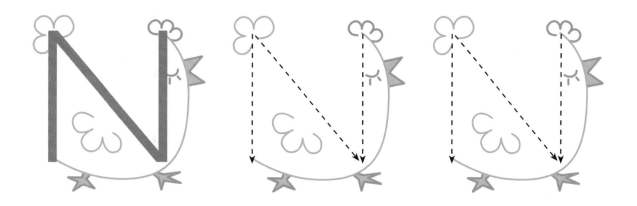

寫一寫
Trace and write

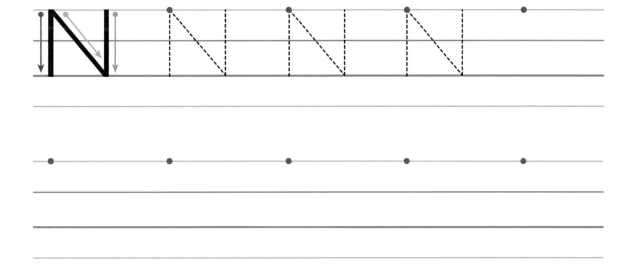

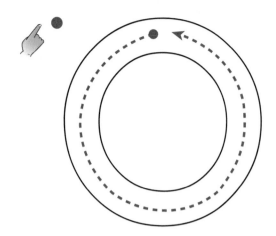

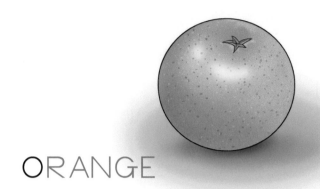

ORANGE

 畫一畫
Trace the Lines

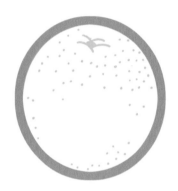 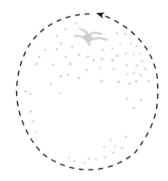 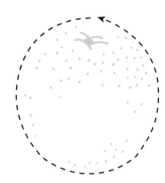

 寫一寫
Trace and write

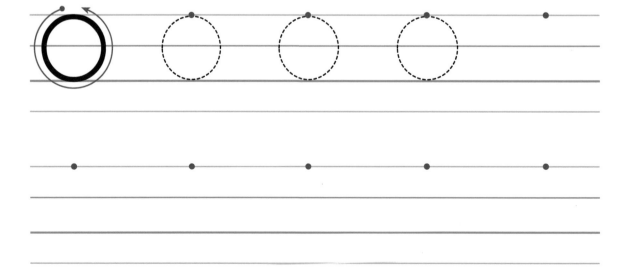

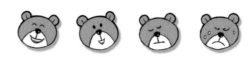

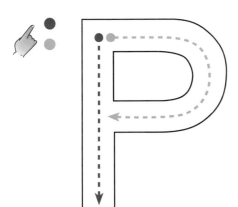

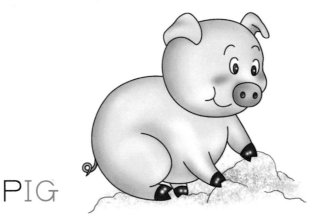

PIG

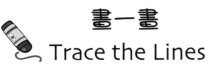
書一畫
Trace the Lines

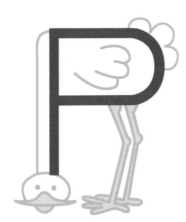 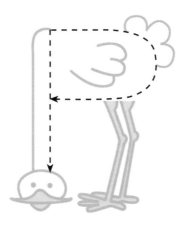 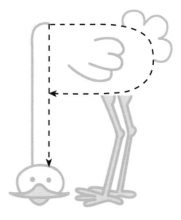

寫一寫
Trace and write

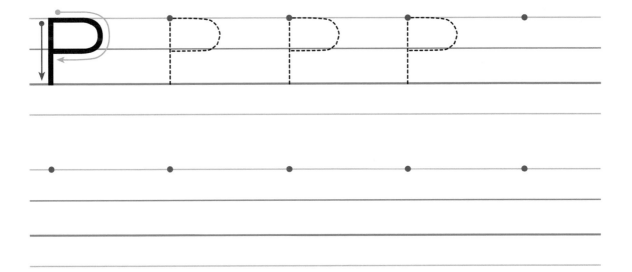

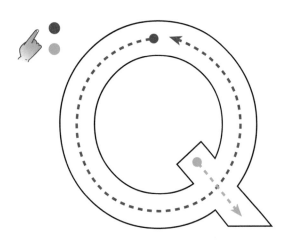

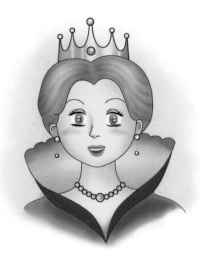

QUEEN

書一畫
Trace the Lines

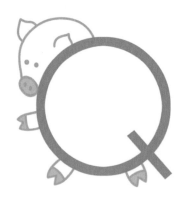 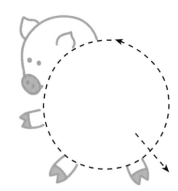 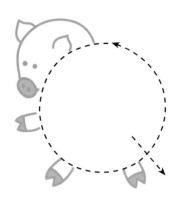

寫一寫
Trace and write

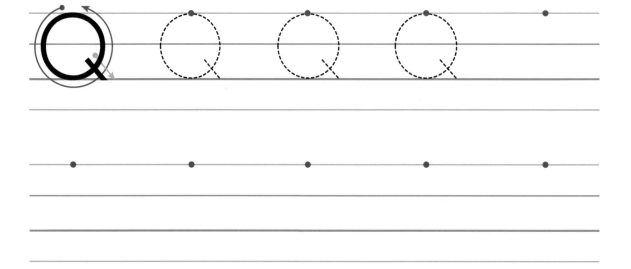

把猴子身上的大楷字母填上顏色。
Colour the capital letters.

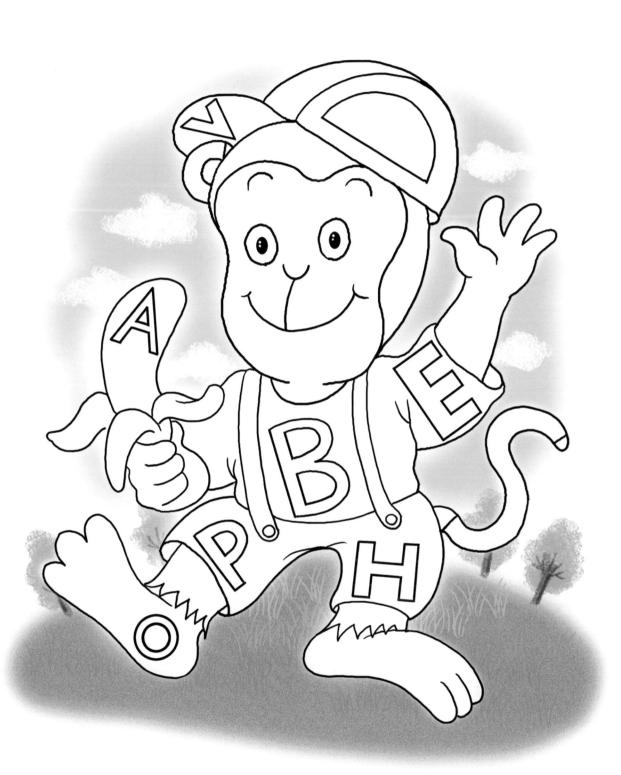

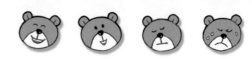

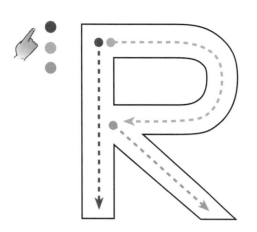

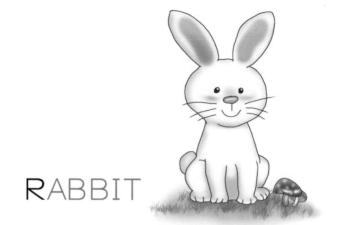

RABBIT

書一畫
Trace the Lines

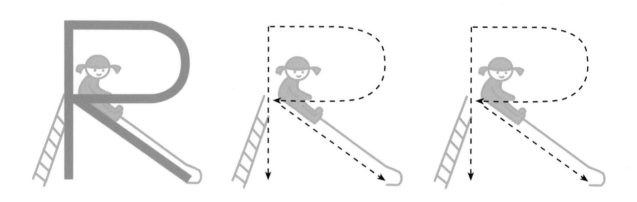

寫一寫
Trace and write

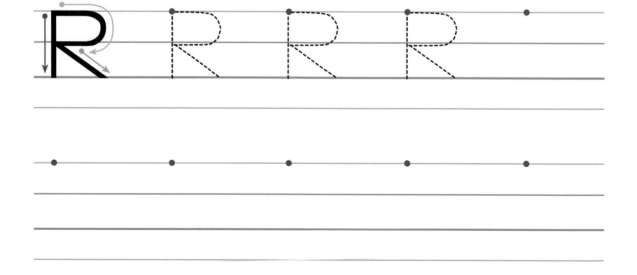

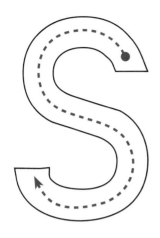

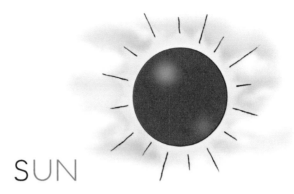

SUN

 畫一畫
Trace the Lines

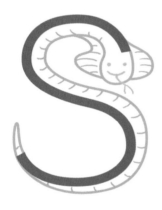 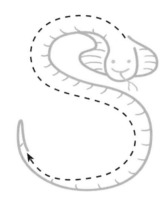 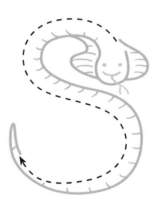

 寫一寫
Trace and write

S S S S

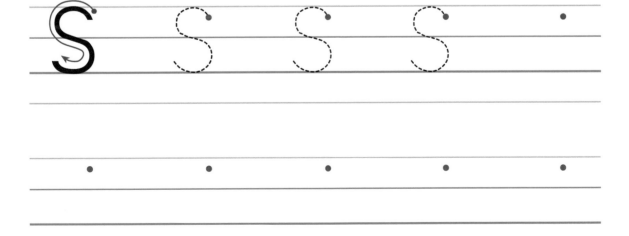

23

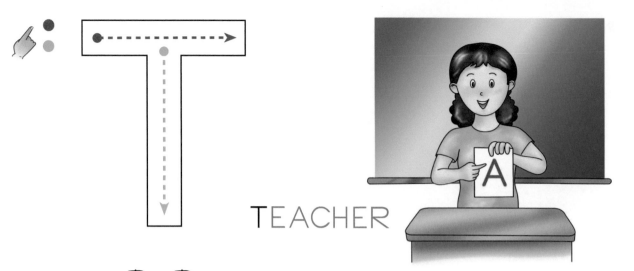

TEACHER

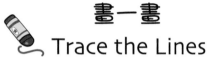

書一畫

Trace the Lines

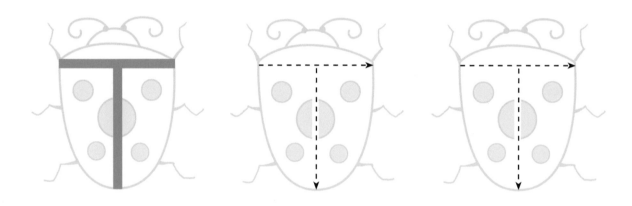

寫一寫

Trace and write

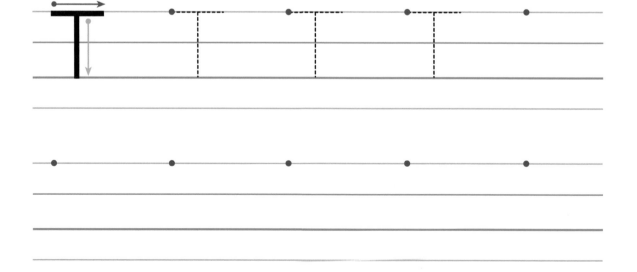

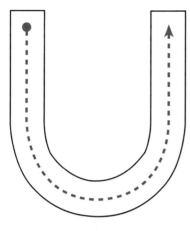

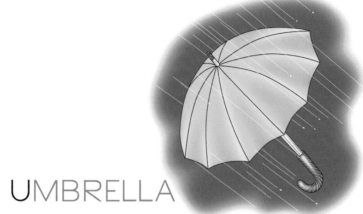

UMBRELLA

畫一畫
Trace the Lines

 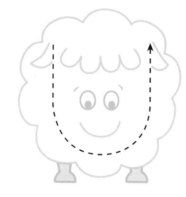 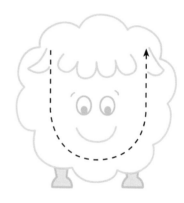

寫一寫
Trace and write

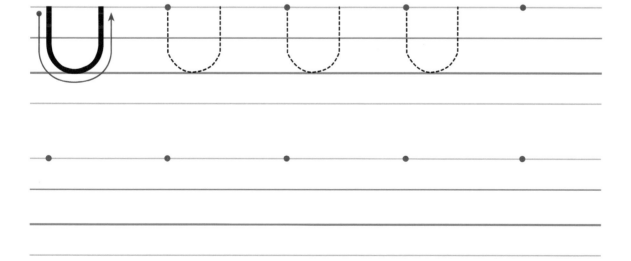

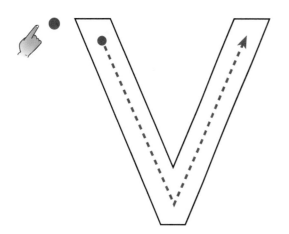

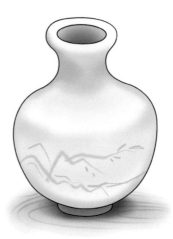

VASE

畫一畫
 Trace the Lines

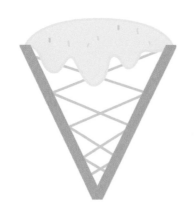 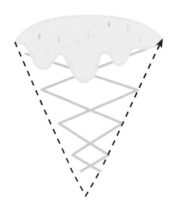 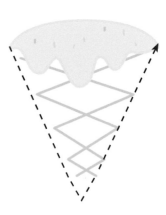

寫一寫
Trace and write

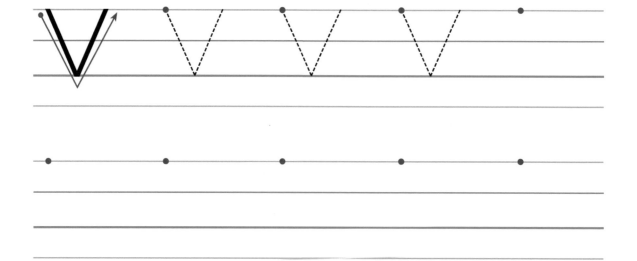

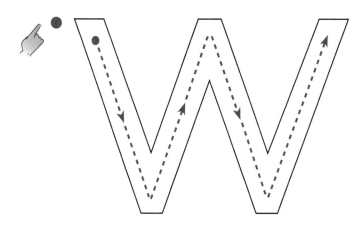

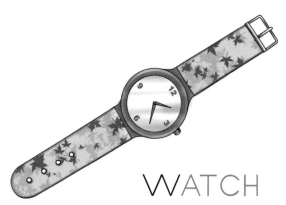

WATCH

畫一畫
Trace the Lines

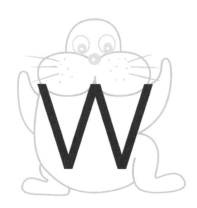 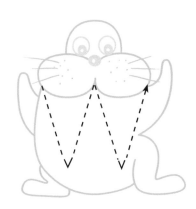 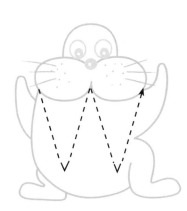

寫一寫
Trace and write

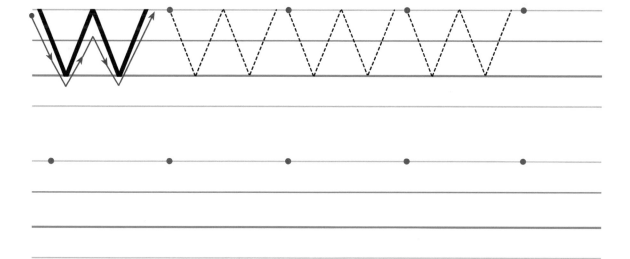

請圈出正確的字。
Please circle the correct words.

	(RABBIT)　　ROSE　　RED
	SEA　　SUN　　SNAKE
	TABLE　　TEACHER　　TREE
	UNDER　　UMBRELLA　　UP
	VAN　　VIOLIN　　VASE
	WIND　　WINDOW　　WATCH

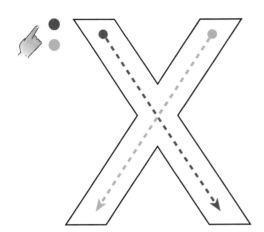

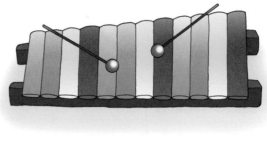

XYLOPHONE

畫一畫
Trace the Lines

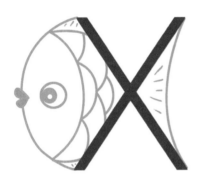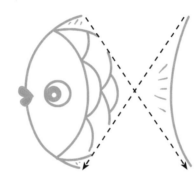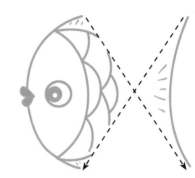

寫一寫
Trace and write

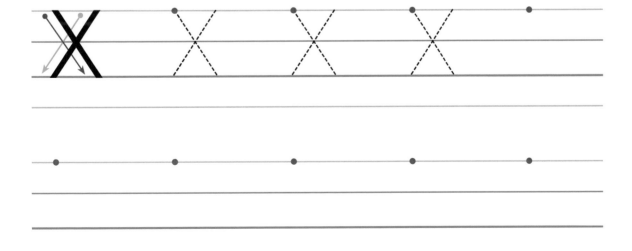

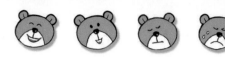

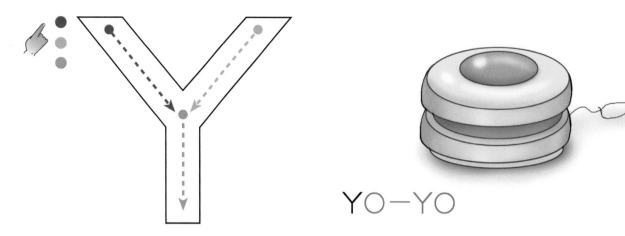

YO–YO

畫一畫
Trace the Lines

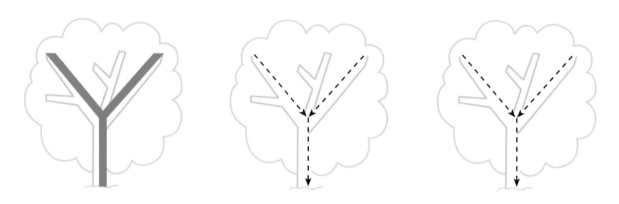

寫一寫
Trace and write

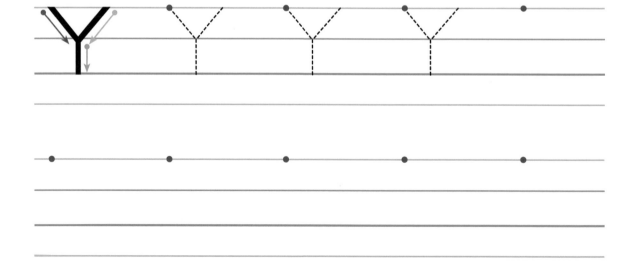

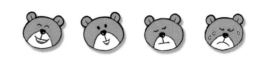

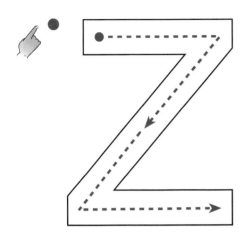

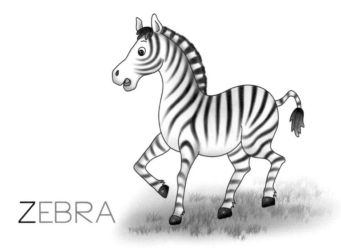

ZEBRA

書一畫

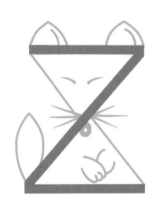 Trace the Lines

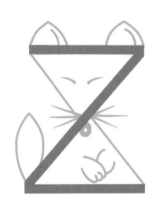
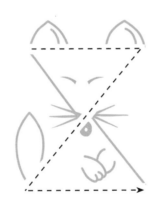
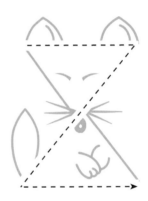

寫一寫

Trace and write

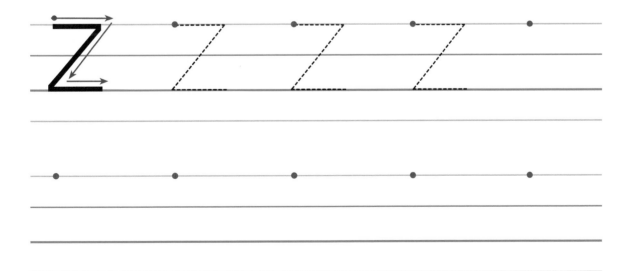

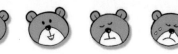

 請順序把Ａ～Ｚ連起來，然後把圖畫填上顏色。
Connect the dots from A~Z. Colour the picture.

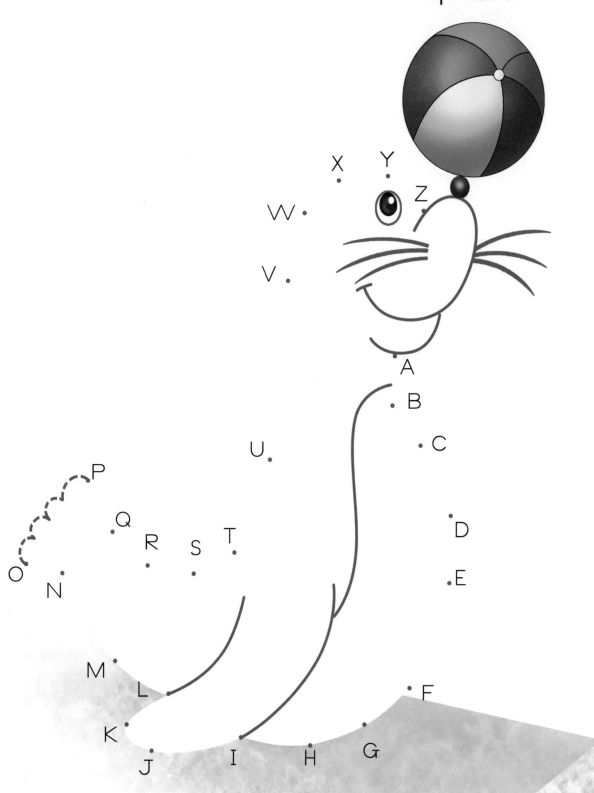